Published by Creative Education
123 South Broad Street, Mankato, Minnesota 56001
Creative Education is an imprint of The Creative Company

Designed by Stephanie Blumenthal.

Photos by: Allsport Photography, Arizona State University,
Associated Press/Wide World Photos, Focus on Sports, Fotosport,
Anthony Neste, Reuters/Corbis-Bettmann,
SportsChrome, and UPI/Corbis-Bettmann.

Library of Congress Cataloging-in-Publication Data

Goodman, Michael E.
Barry Bonds / by Michael E. Goodman.
p. cm. — (Ovations)
ISBN 0-88682-694-2

1. Bonds, Barry, 1964- —Juvenile literature.
2. Baseball players—United States—Biography—Juvenile literature.
[1. Bonds, Barry, 1964- . 2. Baseball players. 3. Afro-Americans—Biography.]
I. Title. II. Series.
GV865.B637G66 1997   93-49767
796.357'092
[B]—DC20

First edition

5 4 3 2 1

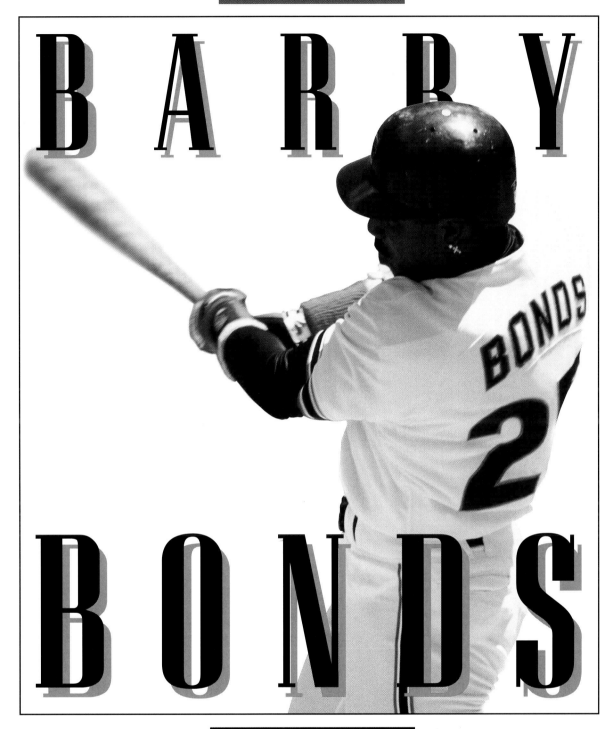

OVATIONS

BARRY

BONDS

BY MICHAEL E. GOODMAN

Creative ℃ Education

REFLECTIONS

Interviewer: Our subject today on "Sports Stars: News and Views" is baseball great Barry Bonds. He has his fans and his critics, and they all have strong views about his talent and personality. We've asked members of our audience for their opinions of Barry, and here are some of their comments:

Fan 1: He's one of the best players in baseball today. He's worth every dollar he's being paid. No one in the National League can match his blend of power, speed, and fielding skill.

Critic 1: He may be a star, but he's not a champion. He has compiled some impressive personal statistics, but his teams have never made it all the way to the top.

Fan 2: Well, he may not have any championship rings yet, but he has helped turn teams in both Pittsburgh and San Francisco into strong contenders. Just having him in the lineup changes the way the opposition plays against Barry's team.

Critic 2: What about the way he treats people after a game? I've seen how he sometimes talks to reporters or fans asking for autographs. He can seem so cold and selfish. Really moody.

Fan 3: That's because he's a private person. He just doesn't feel comfortable in the public eye, at least when he's off the field.

Critic 3: But doesn't he love getting his name into the headlines on the sports pages?

Fan 4: Sure, but he deserves to be there! He's been the best player in the National League throughout the 1990s. He also does a lot of charity work off the field that never makes it into the headlines. I don't think he gets all of the credit he deserves.

Interviewer: As you can see, Barry Bonds is a complex individual—a very private person who is also a talented athlete playing in a public arena. Maybe that's what makes him such a special star.

With his power, speed, and incredible fielding skill, Barry Bonds makes an impression on fans and opponents alike.

EVOLUTION

Some boys dream of being professional baseball players when they grow up. Others hope to follow in their fathers' footsteps, with a career in the same profession. Barry Bonds was able to realize both ambitions because his father, Bobby Bonds, was a star outfielder for the San Francisco Giants during the 1970s.

Barry was born on July 24, 1964, in Riverside, California, and was raised in nearby San Carlos. Growing up with a baseball star as a parent, Barry was involved in the game from the time he was a very little boy. He fell in love with the sport right away, according to his mother, Patricia. "Barry could hit from the first day he lifted a bat at age two. You'd walk in the door and he'd get a bat and ball and make you pitch to him," she remembered. "I knew there was something unique about the way he took to the game."

Barry's parents had just one problem with the boy's hitting ability: sometimes one of his powerful drives would come crashing through a window in the family's home. "It got so I was a regular customer at the W.J. Banks glass store downtown," his mother laughed.

Early on, Barry also developed skills as an outstanding fielder. He learned from the best. One of Barry's favorite activities was visiting his father at work in San Francisco's Candlestick Park (now called 3Com Park). During those visits, he would practice catching fly balls in the outfield. On hand to help him hone his fielding skills were both his father and his godfather, Hall of Famer Willie Mays. "I was six years old and too young to bat with them, but I could compete with them in the field," Barry recalled confidently.

By the time he was a teenager, Barry had become an outstanding baseball, basketball, and football player at Serra High School in San Carlos. He was the school's best athlete, but he wasn't the most popular person. Barry was already displaying a tendency to be somewhat of a loner, with moods that could

Barry Bonds plays for his dad's old team, the San Francisco Giants, where Bobby is a coach.

obscure his exceptional athletic gifts.
"He wasn't cold, but if you weren't
in his inner group, it might seem he
was just keeping to himself," said
his high school basketball coach
Kevin Donahue. "He loved the
limelight though and loved to take
over the game with two minutes to
go," the coach added.

Baseball scouts, in
particular, noticed the young star
with the famous last name. The San
Francisco Giants, his father's old
team, offered Barry $70,000 to sign
a contract when he graduated from
high school. Barry and his parents
talked over the offer and decided
that he should go to college before
becoming a professional baseball
player. So, in the fall of 1982, Barry
enrolled at Arizona State University.

Barry played for three
seasons at ASU,
earning All-Pacific 10 Conference
honors each year. He led the Sun
Devils to the College World Series
during his sophomore year (1983),
and tied an NCAA record in the
series with seven consecutive hits.
Despite his outstanding play, ASU
did not win the national title that
year. It was the first of several

Barry fell in love with baseball when he was a child and his father, Bobby Bonds, was a star player. In college, Barry led the Arizona State University Sun Devils to the College World Series.

failures Barry has experienced
in championship competitions.
He kept up his own fine level of
individual play, however, and was
named to the *Sporting News*
All-America Team as a junior.

In 1985, Barry and his family decided he was ready
for pro baseball. The Pittsburgh
Pirates had made the young man its
first draft choice that year, and he
signed a contract with the club. He
played half a season with the Pirates'
minor league team in Prince William,
Virginia, and moved the next year
to Pittsburgh's top minor
league club in Hawaii.

He didn't stay there long, either—not after Pirates general manager Sid Thrift went to scout Barry early in the season.

"During batting practice, I saw Barry pull five or six balls over the right-field fence. I told him any good left-handed hitter can do that, but I'd like to see him hit a few over the left-field fence," Thrift recalled. "He hit five in a row there and said, 'Is that good enough for you?' I took him back to Pittsburgh with me that night."

After only 115 games in the minors, Barry Bonds was a major leaguer.

He got off to a rocky start in his first season in Pittsburgh, striking out more than 100 times in 113 games. Nearly all of the Pirates had a bad year in 1986. The team finished in last place, 44 games behind the world champion New York Mets.

In 1987, however, things began to improve. Bonds had a lot to do with the change, as did Bobby Bonilla, who, like Bonds, had arrived in Pittsburgh the previous season. Together, the two players were known as the "BB Boys." They not only played well together, they also became best friends. Led by Bonds and Bonilla, the Pirates improved to fourth place in 1987, though still 15 games behind the league-leading St. Louis Cardinals.

At the same time that his professional life was improving, Barry's personal life also became more complete. During a road trip to Montreal, he met a young Swedish woman named Susann, "Sun" for short. The two dated for a while and then married. Though the couple stayed together only eight years before divorcing in 1995, their two children, Nikolai and Shakira, remain a central part of Barry's life.

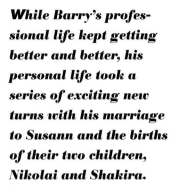

While Barry's professional life kept getting better and better, his personal life took a series of exciting new turns with his marriage to Susann and the births of their two children, Nikolai and Shakira.

Barry's commitment to his children spilled over into a strengthened commitment to develop his baseball talent. He led the Pirates to a second-place finish in 1988 and then to a string of three straight National League Eastern Division titles from 1990-92. During that three-year span, no player in the National League could equal Barry's performance in the regular season. He batted over .300 and averaged more than 30 home runs, 110 runs batted in, and 40 stolen bases a year. He was twice named the National League's Most Valuable Player—in 1990 and 1992—and finished a close second in the voting in 1991 to Terry Pendleton of the Atlanta Braves. In addition, Barry won the Gold Glove each year as the best defensive left fielder in the league.

Despite Barry's outstanding personal statistics, some baseball writers and fans criticized him for underachieving when the pressure was on. The problem was that the Pirates lost in the National League

Championship Series (NLCS) to the Western Division champs each season, thus failing all three times to earn a berth in the World Series. As team leader, Barry was the person who took the most blame for Pittsburgh's playoff failures. And, in some ways, he deserved it. Barry played miserably in the 1990 and 1991 NLCS, batting under .160 with no home runs and only one RBI. He did only slightly better in 1992.

Barry was as upset and mystified as anyone else about his playoff problems. "How can you be so good and do so well for 162 games, and then all of a sudden disappear?" he asked. "But I can only do my best, and I go out there and try my best."

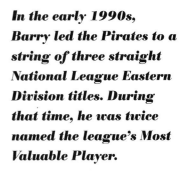

In the early 1990s, Barry led the Pirates to a string of three straight National League Eastern Division titles. During that time, he was twice named the league's Most Valuable Player.

The 1992 season—the club's third near-miss for the National League pennant—was the most trying one for Bonds. He felt particularly lonely that year because Bobby Bonilla, his best friend, had left Pittsburgh to sign as a free agent with the New York Mets before the season began.

Despite Bonilla's absence in 1992, the Pirates fooled most of the baseball experts and raced to their third straight division title. For the second time in his career, Barry made the "30-30 Club" with more than 30 home runs and 30 stolen bases in the same season. That is a familiar club for the Bonds family. Barry's father, Bobby Bonds, became a member a record five times during his playing days.

The season came down to a seven-game struggle between the Pirates and the Atlanta Braves in the National League Championship Series. With two outs in the ninth inning of the seventh game, the Pirates held a one-run lead. Atlanta had runners on second and third and a pinch hitter at bat. CRACK! The ball was lined to Barry's left for a clean hit. One runner scored to tie the game, while the second raced toward the plate. Nearly

Bobby Bonilla, left, and Barry Bonds were known as the "BB Boys" while in Pittsburgh. As teammates and best friends, the energetic duo led the Pirates on an upward climb in the league standings.

every fan in the Atlanta
stadium stood to watch
the drama as Barry
fielded the ball and tried
to make a perfect throw
home to get the runner
out and keep the Braves
from winning.

Barry's throw
made the
catcher move slightly out of
position, and both the runner
and catcher dove toward the plate
at the same time. The umpire shout-
ed "SAFE!" The Pirates had failed
to win the pennant once again.

"When I made that throw,
I thought the runner was out,"
Barry said. "They still say he was
safe, but I still think he was out.
When I keep looking at the tape,
you really can't tell. But he could
have been safe. You don't know if
his foot was down or not. But it's
over with now."

Barry's career in Pittsburgh was also over. When team officials told him, "You're just too expensive for us," Barry began talking to other teams about a new contract. The Giants offered Bonds a six-year deal for what was then a record $43 million. He readily accepted for two reasons: he felt he deserved to be one of the highest-paid players in baseball, and he welcomed the chance to come "home" again and play in the city and stadium in which he had grown up.

To make his homecoming complete, Barry chose to wear his father's old number 25. "I can always remember as a kid this number 25 and this number 24 (his godfather Willie Mays) in the outfield," Barry commented. "It's like rewinding a tape. When I go in the gap for a ball now, it's like my dad and Willie will still be playing the game, because I'm carrying both of them with me."

After the 1992 season, Barry signed with the San Francisco Giants. As a tribute to his father, Barry chose to wear the number 25—his father's old number. It's like my dad...will still be playing the game.

Barry's presence helped turn a San Francisco team that had been mediocre in 1992 into a pennant contender in 1993. The Giants raced out to a big lead in the National League Western Division early in the year, but lost out to the Atlanta Braves on the last day of the season. For the fourth year in a row, Barry's team had come up just a little bit short.

The team may not have accomplished all it could in 1993, but Barry showed his critics that he was worth the huge salary he received from the Giants. He recorded his best offensive statistics ever (.336 batting average, 46 home runs, and 123 runs batted in), and won his third MVP trophy in four years by a landslide vote of the baseball writers. In a survey taken a few months after the season ended, National League managers voted Barry the league's "most exciting player" as well.

The move back to San
Francisco also mellowed
Barry personally. He became involved with several local charities,
particularly an organization called
Adopt a Special Kid (AASK),
which places special-needs children
in caring homes. Barry regularly
purchases large blocks of tickets
for these children in a section of
3Com Park and donates $100 to
AASK for each home run, stolen
base, and RBI he records.

Those donations have been
piling up over the last few seasons,
as Barry has continued to be among
league leaders in both power and
speed. He recorded his third "30-
30" season in 1995, and early in
1996 passed another key milestone
by becoming only the fourth player
in major league history to hit more
than 300 home runs and steal more
than 300 bases. The other three

players in this select group are his father, his godfather, and Andre Dawson. Bonds finished the 1996 season with more than 40 home runs and 100 runs batted in—posting another exceptional year.

During the first six seasons of the 1990s, Barry Bonds has maintained a .308 batting average, with 35 home runs, 107 RBI, and 37 stolen bases per year. What makes those numbers even more amazing is that Barry has been walked more than 100 times each season by National League pitchers afraid to let him hit. He has also been the best batter in the National League in late innings or close games. "He's probably more comfortable in clutch situations than he is with nobody on in the first inning," said teammate Matt Williams.

Barry has even made an effort to be a less private person off the diamond. That has meant being nicer to fans seeking autographs and to writers hoping to interview him. "You have to relax and let people get close to you," advised Tony Gwynn of the San Diego Padres, who is both a friend and a fellow

Barry Bonds became the fourth player in major league history to hit more than 300 home runs and steal more than 300 bases. The other three players are from left, his godfather, Willie Mays, his father, Bobby, and Andre Dawson.

All-Star. Bonds has tried to follow Gwynn's advice and admits that his life "is a lot different and better now." He still isn't considered the friendliest player in the league, but he's getting over his reputation as one of the least cooperative.

What does the future hold for Barry Bonds? He's hoping to wear a World Series ring one day. Then he will have proved to everyone else what most major league players already know. As Brett Butler of the Los Angeles Dodgers put it, "There is no doubt that Barry Bonds is the best player in baseball."

Barry Bonds, the National League's top batter in late innings or close games, is also the best paid. He agreed to a 1997 contract extension for $11.45 million—the highest average salary in major league baseball.

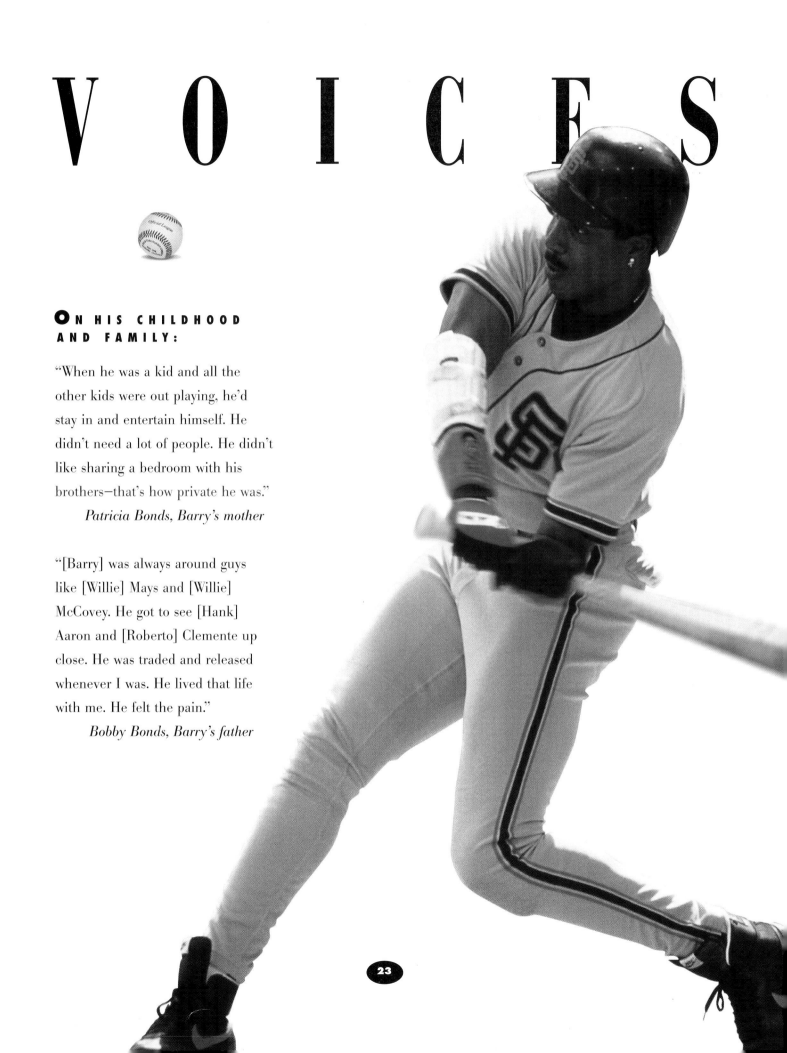

VOICES

ON HIS CHILDHOOD
AND FAMILY:

"When he was a kid and all the
other kids were out playing, he'd
stay in and entertain himself. He
didn't need a lot of people. He didn't
like sharing a bedroom with his
brothers—that's how private he was."
Patricia Bonds, Barry's mother

"[Barry] was always around guys
like [Willie] Mays and [Willie]
McCovey. He got to see [Hank]
Aaron and [Roberto] Clemente up
close. He was traded and released
whenever I was. He lived that life
with me. He felt the pain."
Bobby Bonds, Barry's father

"My dad hardly ever saw me play until I was in college. He was always working. I missed out having him there. I understood why he wasn't there, but I didn't like it."

Barry Bonds

"I'm real proud of him. I call him whenever he does something good to tell him how proud I am of him. I've been on the phone a lot lately."

Patricia Bonds

"You know what I'm proudest of? That now I'm known as Barry Bonds's father."

Bobby Bonds

ON HIS TALENT:

"His baseball instincts are unbeliev-able. And he's not just trying to get a hit, he's trying to crush the ball. If you make a bad pitch, he'll hit a home run and he'll embarrass you."

Jeff Brantley, major league pitcher

"I think he's the best player in baseball. It doesn't bother me that he hasn't produced in the postsea-son. Ninety percent of Barry Bonds is better than a hundred percent of most players."

Joe Morgan, ESPN commentator and former baseball star

"Barry Bonds belongs in a higher league."

Jeff Torborg, opposing manager

"He sees things quicker than any other player except Hank Aaron. He sees a pitcher flaring his glove on a change-up and he'll come back to the dugout and point it out. Other guys don't see that kind of thing until the sixth inning, if they see it at all. And once you see it, you'll always be able to see it."

Dusty Baker, Giants manager

Joe Morgan, top photo, and Dusty Baker, center, have high praise for Barry Bonds's abilities.

ON HIS DESIRE FOR PRIVACY:

"All he's ever wanted—it's like his religion—is to be judged by what he's done on the field."

Andy Van Slyke,
former Pirates teammate

"Why can't the people just enjoy the show and let the entertainer go home and get his rest so he can put on another show? But in baseball, you get to see us, touch us, trade our cards, buy and sell our jerseys. To me it dilutes the excitement."

Barry Bonds

"Of all the superstars I've met, popularity wasn't important to them. Barry just wants to play baseball. He's not pushing ballots for popularity."

Bobby Bonds

"To me, when people say I have an attitude problem, it gives me an edge. It makes me mad, so I play better."

Barry Bonds

Barry Bonds, one of baseball's most exciting players, hopes to wear a World Series ring one day.

"Sometimes Barry is tough to deal with, but most of the times he's a gentleman. He ain't phony or fake about anything."

Dusty Baker

"Off the field, Bobby Bonds was misunderstood and troubled, angry over the expectations of others and distrustful of the media. Twenty years later, Barry is living the same life."

Nick Peters, sportswriter

Barry Bonds likes to keep his private life private. He expresses himself in his game, and he wants people to judge him by what they see on the field.

"Tell me something I can't do, and I'll show you I can do it."

Barry Bonds

"I can remember when I was about seven years old. I hit a home run over all the kids' heads. From that day on, I knew I could play the game. I didn't know how far I was going to go, but I knew I was going to be a baseball player or some kind of athlete."

Barry Bonds

"My workout program [exercising and weight training] right now is five hours per day. My father can't believe what I go through to stay in shape. But you can lift weights until you're blue in the face—it doesn't guarantee success."

Barry Bonds

"He has a lot of talent, and he's so good because he works so hard at it. Even in Little League, when he was the best player, it was because he practiced all the time, and he practiced hard. If he felt he was lacking in something, he'd work at it until he got it right. And he loves to win. He's driven by that."

Bobby Bonds

Barry Bonds has always been proud of his father, looking to his many achievements as a source of inspiration. Now, Bobby Bonds, who was once hailed as one of baseball's greatest players, tells people that he is proud to be known as Barry Bonds's father.

OVATIONS